50 THINGS

EVERY YOUNG

GENTLEMAN

SHOULD KNOW

Other GentleManners™ Books

How to Be a Gentleman
John Bridges

A Gentleman Entertains
John Bridges and Bryan Curtis

As a Gentleman Would Say
John Bridges and Bryan Curtis

A Gentleman Gets Dressed Up
John Bridges and Bryan Curtis

A Gentleman Walks Down the Aisle
John Bridges and Bryan Curtis

Toasts and Tributes
John Bridges and Bryan Curtis

50 Things Every Young Gentleman Should Know
Kay West with John Bridges and Bryan Curtis

50 Things Every Young Lady Should Know
Kay West with John Bridges and Bryan Curtis

How to Be a Lady
Candace Simpson-Giles

As a Lady Would Say
Sheryl Shade

How to Raise a Gentleman
Kay West

How to Raise a Lady
Kay West

A Lady at the Table
Sheryl Shade with John Bridges and Bryan Curtis

A Gentleman at the Table
John Bridges and Bryan Curtis

A Gentleman Abroad
John Bridges and Bryan Curtis

50 THINGS

EVERY YOUNG

GENTLEMAN

SHOULD KNOW

REVISED AND EXPANDED

WHAT TO DO,
WHEN TO DO IT & WHY

JOHN BRIDGES | BRYAN CURTIS

HARPER
HORIZON

Published by Harper Horizon, an imprint of HarperCollins Focus LLC.

Any internet addresses, phone numbers, or company or product information printed in this book are offered as a resource and are not intended in any way to be or to imply an endorsement by HarperCollins, nor does HarperCollins vouch for the existence, content, or services of these sites, phone numbers, companies, or products beyond the life of this book.

Illustrations by Alicia Adkerson, Adkerson Design
Cover Design by Jamie DeBruyn

ISBN 978-1-4016-0382-3 (hard cover)
ISBN 978-1-4016-0650-3 (ebook)

Printed in the United States of America

22 23 24 25 TRM 5 4 3 2 1

CONTENTS

INTRODUCTION

More than once, your mom or your dad has probably told you, "Sit up straight. Act like a gentleman."

You know what they mean. They want you to have nice manners. They want you to be a young man people like. They want you to be a young man people trust. They want you to be a young man people respect. They want you to be a young man who gets into good schools and gets a good job.

Being a gentleman does not mean that you can't have a good time. In fact, it can be fun—and a big relief—to know how to do things the right way. But there are a number of rules you will want to follow if you want to behave in a gentlemanly way.

You probably know a lot of these rules already. You know that a gentleman does not smack his chewing gum or stick it under the seat of his chair. You know that a gentleman does not chew with his mouth open or make irritating noises with his armpits. You know that a gentleman is helpful to older people and that he offers to help clear the table after dinner is finished.

But there are other rules, too, and a lot of them are included in this book. They are not difficult to follow, but you may need to practice them a little so they will come easily to you.

If you start now, however, they will stick with you for years to come. Then, when you are older, people will look at you and say, "Well, isn't he a fine gentleman?"

Better yet, there may be an immediate payoff for all this hard work. It may mean the best summer job you've ever had. It may mean impressing your friends. It may even mean impressing your parents so much that you get more privileges.

We hope you enjoy this book. We hope it brings you lots of good friends and lots of great times. We hope it will help you make your parents proud.

Chapter 1

SAYING "PLEASE"

Saying "please" is the simplest thing you will ever have to do. It is like taking the easiest class at your school. It is a slam dunk. It's probably smart to start using the word "please" as often as you can, beginning right now. It will make life go much more smoothly for you.

Here's what's in it for you: Remember when you were three or four and you would ask for something, and before your mom would give it to you, she would stand there asking, "What do you say?" and of course you would say, "Pleeeeeeeeease." And she would give it to you. That was cute when you were three. But look how old you are now.

If you haven't already started using "please" all the time, you should be worried. And your parents certainly ought to be concerned. They may even be asking themselves, "Should we even bother putting him in the will?"or "Why should we be worrying about sending him to college? He can't even say 'please.'"

Start practicing now:

At the breakfast table, you don't say, "Can I have some cereal?"

Instead, you say, "May I have some cereal, please?"

If somebody asks, "Do you want sugar on your cereal?" you don't say, "Yeah."

Instead, you say, "Yes, please."

If you're on a crowded elevator, you don't say, "Can somebody over there press nine?"

Instead, you say, "Would someone press nine, please?"

If you come to the door, and your hands are full, you don't say, "Hey! Somebody get the door!" Instead, you say, "Would you hold the door open for me, please?"

"Please" is a lot the newest gaming system and having cash in your pocket. It makes the world a nicer place to live in.

Learn how to use it, and start using it now. It will take you far.

You do

Say "please" any time you are asking someone to do something for you. That means, when you're in a restaurant, you say to the waiter, "May I have another soda, please?"

You don't

Assume, just because other people are doing their jobs, that you don't have to show appreciation for their efforts.

Why

One day you will realize that you should be as nice to the person who opens the door for you as you would be to the president. If you learn that now, you will be way ahead of the game.

A gentleman knows that "please" and "thank you" go together like nachos and cheese.

———

A gentleman says "please" to anyone offering him assistance. It does not matter if he is being offered an order of fries or free tickets to a football game.

Chapter 2

SAYING "THANK YOU"

Saying "Thank you" is just as easy—and as important—as saying "please." Remember how easy it was to play T-ball? Saying "thank you" is that easy. You say, "Thank you," any time anyone does something nice or helpful for you.

When someone holds an elevator door open for you—you say, "Thank you."

When someone tells you that you are the smartest young man they have ever met—you say, "Thank you."

When someone gives you a new video game—you say, "Thank you."

When someone hands you a saltshaker—you say, "Thank you."

You do

Say, "Thank you," whenever anybody says something nice to you—even if you are not sure you're being paid a compliment.

You don't

Ask, "Is that supposed to be a compliment?"

Why

When people tell you that you look just like your grandfather, they are trying to say something nice. Even if you don't think being compared to someone who has lost most of his hair is a compliment—it is. Just say, "Thank you." It will make your grandfather very happy.

You do

Say, "Thank you," whenever someone gives you a gift, even if you are not crazy about it.

You don't

Laugh or frown or do anything else that gives the impression that you do not like the gift.

Why

You are not always going to like every gift you receive. Every young gentleman has an aunt who gives him underwear or a godparent who buys him things that are four years too young for him. But it is always important to say, "Thank you." You don't have to pretend that you love something you don't like. But saying, "Thank you for thinking of me," gets the job done. And you are still letting people know that you appreciate them and their thoughtfulness.

YOU DO

Say, "Thank you," when your mom hands you your allowance, when the person behind the counter at the fast food restaurant gives you your chicken nuggets, and when your dad helps you with your homework.

YOU DON'T

Assume, just because you're used to getting your allowance, picking up your chicken nuggets, or having help with your homework, that you don't need to say, "Thanks."

Why

It is important to be nice to people who do nice things for you—whether it is fixing your dinner or smiling when they hand you your chicken nuggets. When people treat you well and they see you behaving like a gentleman in return, they will be proud to know their efforts haven't been lost on you.

A gentleman does not put a price tag on his saying "thank you." He says, "Thank you," for small acts of kindness, just as he does for the big ones.

———

A gentleman knows that a simple "Thank you" is usually fine. There is never any need to go on and on.

Chapter 3

SAYING "EXCUSE ME"

Whether you are stepping in front of someone in a store, or sneezing or burping, or trying to get another person's attention, "Excuse me" is a phrase you will need to use for the rest of your life.

It doesn't matter whether you are a young man or an old man. You are going to burp or pass gas or get the hiccups. You are going to have to step around other people on airplanes, at the movies, or in the bleachers at a ball game. You are going to have to interrupt someone to ask a question or ask for help. It just happens.

Saying "Excuse me" is the right thing to do, in all these situations. It doesn't matter whether you're getting in someone else's space, whether you've created an odor that smells like a dead animal, or whether you need to interrupt somebody to ask for directions. "Excuse me" is always the right thing to say.

You don't need to say, "I'm sorry," because you haven't done anything wrong—unless you have been rude and walked in front of somebody at the movies and stood there so long he or she missed half the show. That's when you need to say, "I'm sorry." But most of the time, "Excuse me" is all you need to say.

You do

Try to wait until you can get outdoors before you pass gas. At least try to get to a room where you will be the only one breathing the air for a while.

You don't

Assume, just because you can say, "Excuse me," that it's Okay for you to pass gas, no matter where you are.

Why

Accidents happen. But if it's not an accident, you're just being rude, and it won't take long for people to figure out that they don't want to be trapped in a room with you.

You do

Say, "Excuse me," when you have to interrupt someone, like the librarian at your school who may be reading a book (that's what librarians do), to ask for help in locating the book you need for your homework.

You don't

Just stand around and wait fifteen minutes, hoping the librarian will finally notice you standing there.

Why

It is perfectly all right to ask a question. "Excuse me" was invented for moments like this—when you need to get someone's attention.

A gentleman never uses the words "Hey," "Hey you," "Hey dude," or any phrase that starts with the word "hey" when he is trying to get another person's attention. He says, "Excuse me."

———

A gentleman does his best to control all bodily functions in public. That way, he will not have to say "Excuse me" all the time.

Chapter 4

MAKING AN APOLOGY

There are plenty of times in life when you will want to say, "I'm sorry." When we make mistakes, it is best to go ahead and admit them. You may need to say, "I'm sorry I hurt your feelings," "I'm sorry I left my pocket knife on the couch and you sat on it," "I'm sorry I used the last of the toilet paper and forgot to put in a new roll," or even "I'm sorry I spit in the air and the wind caught it and it hit you in the face."

You probably can make your own list of times when you will need to say, "I'm sorry"—because everybody makes mistakes and does stupid things. A gentleman tries to make as few mistakes as possible, and if you are lucky, as you get older, you won't make mistakes quite so often. If you try not to make the same mistakes twice, you will be relieved that you don't have to say, "I'm sorry," again and again. Better yet, people will accept your apologies and forgive you for having screwed up.

YOU DO

Say, "I'm sorry," and mean it.

YOU DON'T

Say, "I'm sorry," if you don't really mean it or if you're just trying to get somebody off your back. People are smarter than you think; they know a phony apology when they hear one.

Why

Being a good guy means that you admit it when you do things that hurt or inconvenience other people.

YOU DO

Say more than "I'm sorry" if the occasion calls for it. For example, if you throw a baseball and smash the neighbor's window, you say, "I'm sorry I broke your window. I'll make sure it gets replaced." If you can't afford to pay for something you have broken, you can offer to work out an arrangement that will allow you to correct your mistake. Maybe you can work out a deal with your parents so that they will give you an advance on your allowance, or maybe they will let you do some extra work around the house to earn the money you need.

You don't

Assume that saying "I'm sorry" always gets you off the hook.

Why

A gentleman knows that sometimes a few words are not enough to fix a mistake. Part of growing up is learning what you really need to do when you've damaged somebody's property or hurt another person's feelings.

A gentleman, who has offended another person, says, "I'm sorry."

———

A gentleman does his best not to offend anyone on purpose, but if he realizes that he has offended another person because he didn't think before he spoke or acted, he immediately apologizes.

———

A gentleman knows that saying "I'm sorry" will not mean much if he does not try to do better. You can only get away with forgetting to feed the dog so many times before your parents, and the dog, start growling at you.

Chapter 5

ACCEPTING AN APOLOGY

Let's say a friend's dog has chewed up a book you let your friend borrow. The friend says, "I'm sorry." You might respond in one of two ways. You might say, "That's okay. Stuff like that happens." Or you might say, "You idiot. Why did you leave my book lying around where your dumb dog could eat it?"

Sometimes, it's hard to say, "I accept your apology." But most of the time it is the right thing to do. Because you want to do the gentlemanly thing, you try to put yourself in your friend's place. If it had been your dog that destroyed your friend's property, you would feel miserable. You would hope that your friend would give you a break, so you try to cut him some slack as well.

If your brother forgets to replace the toilet paper roll after he has used the last of it and he says, "My bad. I'm sorry," you accept the apology. Similarly, if the server in a restaurant brings you a sandwich you didn't order, and he says, "I'm sorry. Let me make that right," you accept the apology. After all, that's what you'd want them to do for you.

YOU DO

Forgive someone when he or she says, "I'm sorry." Then you move along, as if the mistake never happened.

YOU DON'T

Let yourself be taken advantage of. If your friend's dog chews up your book every time you loan him one, you may still accept his apology—but you don't have to loan him any more books.

Why

Being a gentleman does not mean you have to let people treat you badly. Sometimes, if someone does the same inconsiderate things or hurts your feelings over and over again, you may want to keep your distance from them.

You do

Say, "That's okay," when someone apologizes.

You don't

Say, "That's okay, just don't let it happen again," or "That's okay, but try not to be so stupid next time."

Why

It's not fair to pretend to accept a person's apology and still try to make that person feel rotten. When you accept an apology, it's best to use as few words as possible—especially if, deep inside, you're still feeling angry or upset.

A gentleman knows how to
forgive and forget.

———

A gentleman does not keep reminding his friends about their past mistakes. If he finds that he is getting tired of the same old problems occurring, he might want to think about getting new friends.

Chapter 6

INTRODUCING YOUR FRIENDS TO YOUR PARENTS

Your parents don't want to run your life. But they do have the right to ask a few questions.

Let's say they run into you at the mall or in the park, and see you talking to someone they do not know. If you just wave at your mom or dad and then go on talking with your friend, your parents may be thinking, "That's a cute girl. I wonder if she's his girlfriend? I bet she'd make a lovely daughter-in-law and their children would be beautiful." Or they may be thinking, "That kid looks like trouble. I think I saw him on the ten o'clock news last night." Or they might be thinking, "This child I raised from a baby has no manners. I have failed terribly." (And that would be the worst thing possible.)

You don't want them thinking any of these

things—especially about the girl. But it can be easy to nip that idea in the bud.

You definitely don't want your parents coming over to you and saying something like, "Scott must not want us to meet you. Just how do you know our son?" Or "Our son obviously has no manners. Hi, I'm Scott's mom." Or the worst: "Well, since Scott won't introduce us, I will just have to assume that you are his girlfriend."

You can stop all of this very easily if you just start introducing your friends to your parents. It is really painless, and, if you do it right away, they'll have less time to think of something to say that will embarrass you.

You do

Say, "Dad, this is Michael. He's on my baseball team." Or "Mom, I'd like you to meet Jessica. We go to school together."

You don't

Just say, "Dad, this is Michael." Or "Mom, this is Jessica."

Why

When you give your parents a little information about your friends, it gives them a chance to say something that doesn't make you feel uncomfortable—something like, "So Michael, what position do you play?" Give your parents a break. They are probably much more interesting than you think, and having parents your friends like is a great thing for you.

You do

Feel free to add something interesting about your parents when you introduce your friends to them. You might say, "My dad used to play third base, too," or "My mom had Mr. Caldwell as a principal. She said he was mean back then, too."

You don't

Assume your parents are simply going to go away once you've made your introduction. They are going to want to get to know your friends.

Why

When you lead the introduction process, you get to control the conversation. That way, there will be a much smaller chance that unfortunate topics, such as your bad report card or girlfriends, will come up. It is good to be in charge, once in a while. This can be the moment when you really impress your parents, and your friends.

A gentleman always introduces the younger person to the older person. He says, "Dad, this is Michael." He does not say, "Michael, this is my dad." That works on every occasion, not just with your parents. For example, it's right to say, "Grandpa, this is Michael." It's wrong to say, "Michael, this is my grandpa."

Chapter 7

SAYING "MA'AM" AND "SIR"

In some parts of the country, young gentlemen are brought up to say "ma'am" and "sir" when they are talking to older people. In other places, people never say "ma'am" or "sir."

If you live in Maine and you are visiting your grandmother in Georgia, you might think it sounds stupid when you hear your cousins saying "ma'am" and "sir." But if you're from Georgia and are visiting your grandmother in Maine, you might think your cousins are being rude when they answer adults by simply saying "yes" or "no."

It is not so important what you say, but how you say it. If what you say is said with kindness and respect, it will be the right thing to say.

You do

Answer questions adults ask you with kindness and respect. "Yes, thank you" or "Yes, sir" are both correct.

You don't

Answer an adult with a simple "Nope" or "Yep."

Why

Every person, not just the adults in your life, deserves a respectful response to questions they ask.

You do

Respect the regional differences among people who live in different parts of the country and the world.

You don't

Make fun of people because their traditions are different from yours or because they speak with an accent that doesn't sound like most of the people you know.

Why

Different is not wrong. It is simply different. If you go through life making fun of everybody who is different from you, you will miss out on a lot of great experiences.

If a gentleman is confused because another person's behavior is different from what he has been taught to do, he does not make fun of that person. He never calls attention to someone else's behavior in a public setting.

————

If a young gentleman does not understand another person's behavior, he asks his parents—or another adult—about it. But he waits until they are in private before he requests an explanation.

Chapter 8

ASKING PERMISSION

You might think that you can stop using the things you've learned in this book once you've left home and are living on your own. Sorry to burst your bubble, but almost everything you learn in this book is something you will need to use throughout your entire life.

You will still need to say "Thank you" and "Excuse me" and write thank you notes and show appreciation for gifts you really don't like.

The same goes for asking permission. You may think that when you get older you won't have to ask permission to do what you want to do.

Wrong.

The only changes will be the type of things that you have to ask permission to do. Right now, you might have to ask your dad if you can go to the movies with your buddies. But your dad may also have to ask your mom if he can go on a golf weekend with his buddies, and your mom may have to ask her boss if she can change her work hours. See, it never changes.

But one thing that you can do now is learn how to ask for permission and how to react appropriately if you don't get what you want. It will work for you for the rest of your life.

You do

Ask anytime you are not sure if something is acceptable for you to do.

You don't

Figure it is easier to beg to be forgiven later, rather than ask permission now.

Why

If you want to stay out an hour later than your normal curfew, it is better to ask beforehand, rather than just staying out and hoping your parents will be okay with it. If you don't ask their permission, you'll be running the risk of worrying them and of being punished for your poor judgment. If you ask permission beforehand, you are showing your parents that you respect them and, at the same time, you are giving them an opportunity to show that they trust you. If you ask them for little things instead of doing things without permission—like staying out for an extra hour—then, when you get older, you'll stand a better chance of getting permission for bigger privileges, like a weekend trip with your friends.

You do

Accept a "no" when you hear it.

You don't

Whine, complain, and moan when you don't get your way.

Why

Your brother may have a good reason for not letting you use his bike. While it might seem unfair, it is best not to make a scene. You also stand a better chance of his saying yes the next time if you accept his refusal calmly, as a gentleman would do.

> A gentleman never simply assumes that it is okay for him to use something that belongs to someone else. He always asks permission.

Chapter 9

PAYING A COMPLIMENT

Everybody likes to hear people saying nice things about him or her. It could be, "Wow. You pitched a great game," or "You did a great job at your bar mitzvah," or "Mom, your new haircut looks great," or "Grandpa, you make the best chocolate cake in the world."

It doesn't cost anything to pay somebody a compliment. But a genuine compliment is one of the best gifts you can give. It doesn't get old or wear out, and it will make somebody happy—somebody who may remember it forever.

YOU DO

Tell someone when you think he or she has done something good.

You don't

Worry that other people will think you are trying to get on somebody's good side, or that you are trying to be the "teacher's pet."

Why

There is nothing wrong with any compliment, as long as you really mean it—even if it's a compliment to your teacher or to your sister. It is always right to say something nice to another person, even if that person is someone you do not know very well.

You do

Pay a compliment only when you really mean it.

You don't

Go around paying compliments to everybody, all the time, so that your compliments don't sound special anymore.

Why

If you like, but don't love, your grandma's apple pie, you don't say it was the best pie you ever tasted. Saying, "Thank you, that was good," is just fine. When your grandma does make your favorite pie, that's the time to tell her how much you like it. The compliment will be much more special if it is genuine—and your grandma will know the difference.

A gentleman does not pay a compliment
he doesn't mean.

———

A gentleman is not afraid to compliment
anyone, male or female, when that person
has done something well.

Chapter 10

ACCEPTING A COMPLIMENT

Do you know one of the biggest mistakes adults make? No, it's not their haircuts or the music they listen to. Or wearing black socks with shorts and sandals—although that is pretty hard to forgive.

One of the biggest mistakes most adults make is that they don't know how to accept a simple compliment.

When somebody says something nice, some people don't know that the right thing to do is to say a simple "Thank you." Maybe they think they are acting humble. But they are wrong. They are actually being rude.

Here are three compliments and the right—and wrong—way to respond to them:

You do

Say, "Thank you," when someone says, "That is a great shirt."

You don't

Say, "I hate it. I am only wearing it because my Aunt Molly bought it for me and she's here for the weekend."

Why

By saying you hate the shirt, you have insulted the taste of the person who paid you the compliment.

You do

Say, "Thank you," when someone says, "I like your haircut."

You don't

Say, "My dad made me get it cut. I hate it this short."

Why

It is rude to disagree with someone who is trying to say something nice about you.

You do

Say, "Thank you, I really worked hard," when someone says, "You did a great job at your bar mitzvah."

You don't

Say, "You must not have been listening when I messed up."

Why

When a person tells you that you have done a good job, it is rude to suggest that the person does not know what he or she is talking about. Even if you know, deep down, that there were moments when you messed up, you don't need to point them out. A simple "Thank you" is all you need to say.

If you see a pattern forming here, you are right. Whenever somebody pays you a compliment, "Thank you" is always the right thing to say.

A gentleman knows that accepting a compliment graciously is just as important as giving a compliment. He knows how to do both.

Chapter 11

KNOWING WHEN TO KEEP YOUR MOUTH SHUT

Although a gentleman tries very hard not to hurt other people's feelings, there probably will come a time when—even without meaning to—he will say the wrong thing and make another person feel bad. When that happens he will feel embarrassed, the other person will feel mistreated, and the gentleman will end up having to say, "I'm sorry."

Most of the time you can avoid that sort of painful situation by being very careful what you say. Many times, that means using discretion, which basically means knowing when to keep your mouth shut. Sometimes, after all, the best course of action is to say nothing at all.

You do

Use discretion when talking about upcoming parties.

You don't

Tell another person about a party if you aren't sure if that person has been invited.

Why

You don't want to run the risk of making the other person feel that he or she has been left out. And you definitely do not want people to think that you are bragging.

You do

Know how to keep a secret.

You don't

Tell your mom that your dad has bought her a diamond necklace for her birthday.

Why

The necklace is your dad's gift to your mom, and he wants it to be a surprise. It is much cooler to be the guy who can keep a secret than the guy who can't keep his mouth shut when he should.

You do

Know when you shouldn't keep a secret.

You don't

Keep your mouth shut when you've learned that
someone is going to do something wrong or
something that could cause someone to be hurt.

Why

If you learn that a friend has been stealing other
people's property, using drugs, or doing anything else
that could get him in trouble or cause other people
to be hurt, it is your responsibility to speak up. You
do not spread rumors, but you do tell your parents, a
teacher, or a counselor that you are concerned about
your friend's behavior.

If a friend asks a gentleman if he
wants to hear a secret, a gentleman
thinks twice before he says yes.

Chapter 12

LISTENING TO AND TALKING TO ADULTS

You are going to have to talk to adults—whether they're your teachers, your parents, your coaches, or the people who run the cash registers at the grocery store. There's no way you can avoid it. But if you're going to have to talk to them, you will need to learn to listen to them, too. Nothing makes adults angrier than trying to talk to a young guy who is so caught up with his video game or his phone that they can't even get his attention. (Well, actually one thing does make them angrier: a young guy who responds to every question by saying, "Huh?" or "What?" or "Nope.")

A gentleman knows if he actually has time for a full-scale conversation. If he is on a deadline for a paper that is due the next day, it's okay for him to say, "Can we talk about this later? I'm way behind on this paper." Watching the same movie for the seventeenth time in a row is not a good excuse for ignoring your grandmother. A gentleman turns off the television and talks to his grandma.

Adults aren't always trying to give you orders and make your life harder. Sometimes they're trying to do something nice for you or offer you some help. That's why it's important to learn to listen.

You do

Remove your earbuds, turn down the television, or take a break from your video game when an adult wants to talk to you.

You don't

Say, "I'm busy now" or "Can't you see I'm busy?" or "I'll get back to you when I'm done."

Why

It's important for you to learn to use the pause button. No matter how busy you think you are, you can always take a break from what you are doing to pay attention to another real live human being. They may need to tell you something important, or they may need to ask you a serious question. Even if what they want to talk about doesn't seem important to you, you can simply say, "Can we talk a little later?" That way, you're showing the adult the same respect you'd like the adult to show you.

You do

Try to take the time to have a real conversation with the adults in your life. Having a real conversation means answering questions, asking questions, and trying to speak in full sentences.

You don't

Use words like "Yeah," "Nope," "What?" and "Huh?" when you're having a conversation with an adult.

Why

At some point you are going to be really glad you got to spend time with the adults in your life, and you will cherish that time. You'll be glad you got to know your parents and grandparents and the other adults who care about you. The only real way you are going to be able to get to know each other is by learning to talk and listen.

A gentleman looks adults in the eye when he is talking to them.

———

A gentleman doesn't try to carry on a conversation while he is staring at the TV, his phone, or a computer.

Chapter 13

SHAKING HANDS

This one really impresses older people. Knowing how to shake hands will make your parents look good—and you should never underestimate how great that can be for you. It also makes you look like someone your friends' parents can trust.

If parents see that you know how to shake hands properly, they will assume that you are more grown-up. They will judge you positively if you know how to present yourself when meeting people or making introductions.

YOU DO

Wait for an older person to offer a handshake before you stick out your hand. (Almost everyone who is going to want to shake your hand is probably going to be older than you.)

You don't

Offer any type of handshake other than a simple, firm but painless grip with a couple of modest pumps.

Why

Most adults are not up on current eight-part handshakes. Stick with the basics with your elders.

You do

Wait for a lady to extend her hand to you before you offer to shake her hand.

You don't

Try to break her hand by grasping her hand too tightly.

Why

There's no telling what type of horrible chores you might have to do for an older woman whose hand you have crushed. You might have to wash her laundry, mow her lawn, or do other horrible things.

You do

Explain to someone who offers his or her hand to you if there's a reason you can't shake hands. It is okay to say, "I've been working on my bike and my hand is covered in grease."

You don't

Shake someone's hand and then apologize for making his or her palm as greasy as yours.

Why

Maybe this person was planning to write you a check or do something else nice for you, and now can't, because you mucked up the person's hand with axle grease.

A gentleman laughs when his grandfather pretends to double over in pain because the young gentleman's handshake is so firm and strong—but only if his grandfather is just pretending.

———

If his grandfather really is in pain, a gentleman doesn't think it's funny. He keeps in mind that he may need to take it easy when shaking hands with some older people.

————

A gentleman does not make any comments if another person's handshake is weak or limp.

————

A gentleman tries to make sure that his own handshake is firm and friendly.

————

If a gentleman is wearing gloves outside and it is very cold, he does not have to remove them before shaking hands.

Chapter 14

MEETING PEOPLE WITH PHYSICAL CHALLENGES

This has probably happened to you already: You have seen someone at the mall, or somewhere else, who has a physical challenge. Or you may have been introduced to a person with a physical challenge. It could be an older person in a wheelchair or a guy your own age who has a prosthetic. It is okay for you to wonder why someone has a bad scar or only has one arm. It is not okay, however, to ask that person, "What happened to you?"

You may feel awkward when you meet a person with a physical challenge. But you should do your best not to stare. Until you know the person well, it is not a good idea to ask questions about his or her challenges.

You do

Say, "It's nice to meet you," when you are introduced to someone with a physical challenge—just the same as when you are introduced to any new acquaintance.

You don't

Say, "What happened to your leg [or your face]?" when you are introduced to a person with a physical challenge.

Why

When you focus on just one aspect of a person's life, you are probably missing out on a lot. How would you feel if every time you met someone, they simply stared at your hair or your nose? What if they asked you, "How did you get so fat?" or "Why are you so skinny?" You know there is a lot more to you than the way you look. It's the same with a person who has a physical challenge.

When a gentleman meets someone with a physical challenge, he never blurts out remarks such as, "I would die if that happened to me."

———

When a gentleman is introduced to someone in a wheelchair, he never asks, "Will you ever be able to walk again?"

———

A gentleman offers any assistance he can to physically challenged people. He offers them the same courtesies he would other people, such as opening doors.

Chapter 15

ACCEPTING A GIFT YOU DON'T LIKE

Underwear

Classical music

Arts and crafts projects

Really thick books

Really thick books about history

Ugly sweaters

Ugly sweaters with snowmen on them

Maybe you can look at this list and say, "I'd love that." Then, good for you. There is nothing wrong with getting a snowman sweater or a thick book or even underwear as a gift if that is something you really want or need. But it may *not* be what you want to find when you open a package on your birthday or at Christmas or Hanukkah. At those times it is important to remember that it is not what is inside the package that matters. What matters is that someone took the time to do something he or she thought was nice for you. That's why it's important to know how to react to that thick book or snowman sweater.

YOU DO

Say, "Thank you," for any gift you receive.

YOU DON'T

Claim to be truly excited by a gift that is not what you wanted. (Saying, "Thank you," is enough. Just make sure you don't roll your eyes and groan and say, "What made you think I wanted an old book about history?")

Why

All you need to do is acknowledge that somebody has been kind to you. Simply saying, "Thank you," and following up with a thank you note (see page 55) is all you are expected to do.

YOU DO

Accept someone's gift gratefully, even if it isn't something you wanted.

You don't

Ask where the gift came from, so that you can take it back and get something you really want.

Why

Simply asking that question makes it clear that you don't like the gift, and that would hurt somebody's feelings, which would be rude. A gentleman is never rude—at least, not on purpose.

A gentleman does not measure the worth of a gift by how much it cost.

———

A gentleman says, "Thank you," for every gift he receives, whether it is something he loves or something he hates.

———

If a gentleman receives a gift he already has, he does not say, "Gee. I've already got one of these." Instead, he simply says "Thank you"–and means it.

———

A gentleman never says, "You shouldn't have," when someone presents him with a gift.

Chapter 16

ACCEPTING A GIFT YOU LIKE

Big checks
The right gift cards
Clothes you really like
A book by your favorite author
Video games you want

If you are lucky, and we bet you are, you have someone in your life who gives really cool presents. It might be an uncle or a godmother or a grandfather or a family friend who always gets it right. Maybe she or he gives presents like the ones listed above. If you have a person like this in your life, count your blessings. It is always exciting to open a package from someone who puts a lot of thought into gifts. Try to learn a lesson from this person, so that, when you are giving gifts, you can give the most thoughtful gifts possible. And, yes, it is cool to love a gift. But there are a few things to keep in mind even when accepting a gift you really, really like.

You do

Say, "Thank you," to the gift giver, as soon as you open the present.

You don't

Start raving about how much you love this gift—especially if somebody else in the room has given a gift you didn't like as much.

Why

It is okay to love a gift, but is not okay to compare one gift with another, especially if both gift givers are sitting there in front of you. If you start comparing gifts, somebody's feelings are bound to get hurt. When you write your thank you note (and you *will* write a thank you note, of course), you can let the gift giver know how much you really like the gift. The thank you note is like a private conversation between you and the person you are sending it to. Nobody else will know what you have said, and nobody's feelings will be bruised.

At his birthday, or at the holidays,
a gentleman does not make a scene
if he does not receive every gift he
has asked for.

————

A gentleman does not brag about the
expensive gifts he has received. He knows
that different families live on different
budgets and have different traditions.

Chapter 17

WRITING A
THANK YOU NOTE

When someone does something nice for you or gives you a gift, you thank that person. It is the right thing to do.

And doing the right thing will always pay off. If you have good manners, your friends' parents will be more likely to be comfortable with your being around their kids. When you get older, good manners will help you get a better job and have a better life.

Writing a thank you note will demonstrate that you have the best manners possible. You will be showing people how much you appreciate them. You are not doing it because your mom and dad are forcing you to. You are doing it because you are a thoughtful guy. And that will really impress people. It will also have a lot to do with what they think of you and how they treat you.

You do

Write a thank you note for gifts you receive.

You don't

Assume that, just because you said, "Thank you," when you opened the gift, you have done enough.

Why

When somebody has put time, effort, or money into giving you a gift, writing a thank you note is the right way to show your appreciation.

You do

Write a thank you note on a note card.

You don't

Write a thank you note on a piece of notebook paper or on your computer, even if you use fancy fonts.

Why

You are not a six-year-old. You are old enough to have your own stationery. If you don't know what type of cards you need, you might ask your parents to help you pick them out. Better yet, ask to get your own supply with your name on it. People will be very impressed.

You do

Write a thank you note to your friend's parents if they took you out to eat at a nice restaurant or on an out-of-town trip.

You don't

Write a thank you note to your friend's parents if they simply made you a grilled cheese sandwich when you were over at their house.

Why

There are limits to how many thank you notes you have to write. You should send a thank you note for special gifts or special acts of kindness. A trip to see a professional hockey game requires a thank you note. A grilled cheese sandwich does not. (You do say, "Thank you," when your friend's mom or dad gives you the sandwich, of course.) If you are wondering whether you need to send a thank you note, ask your parents for their advice.

A gentleman knows that a thank you e-mail does not take the place of a thank you note. It is better than nothing, but not as good as a handwritten note.

Here are a few examples of the type of thank you notes you can send on almost any occasion.

Dear Aunt Kelly,

You know how much I like to skate-board. When I opened your package on my birthday and saw the gift card to my favorite sporting goods store, I was reminded why you are such a great aunt. Thank you very much for thinking of me.

Your nephew,
Ted

Dear Grandma,

Thank you so much for the sweater you gave me for Christmas. I love it and will be wearing it to school a lot. Thank you for such a great gift. I look forward to seeing you soon.

Love,
Teddy

Dear Mr. Kelly,

Thank you for taking me to see the Predators last night. What a great game! I really appreciate getting to go with you and Michael to see my favorite hockey team.

Sincerely,
Ted

Chapter 18

SELECTING A GIFT

Buying a great gift for someone is really not that hard, and it doesn't require a lot of money. If you want to give the right type of gift, all you have to do is listen and pay attention, and then put some effort into buying or making the gift.

YOU DO

Pay attention to what people like and dislike.

YOU DON'T

Give someone a gift just because *you* like it.

Why

The purpose of giving a gift is to show someone that you care about her or him. If your dad likes Elvis and you like rap, you don't give him a rap album.

You do

Spend what you can afford on a gift.

You don't

Think that you have to spend a lot of money to make another person happy.

Why

Your friends and family members don't really care how much you paid for your gift. What they do care about is how much thought you put into it. You might buy the gifts using your allowance or money you have earned, or your parents might slip you some money to help you with your shopping. Either way, you're the one picking out the gift, and it's your thoughtfulness, not the price tag, that counts.

You do

Plan ahead.

You don't

Wait until the last minute to buy a gift.

Why

You know when your mother's birthday is—or at least you should know. (If you aren't already keeping a calendar of birthdays and holidays, start keeping one now.) That way, you will have time to pick out the absolutely perfect gift. So your dad likes Elvis? If you plan ahead, you might be able to put some real effort into finding a cool Elvis gift your dad didn't even know about. Let's say your sister especially likes a certain movie actor. If you plan ahead, you might be able to go online and find an autographed picture of him. If you wait until the last minute, you will probably end up grabbing a gift that you haven't really thought about. And you might even forget to remove the price tag.

A gentleman puts some effort into presenting his gifts. He does his best when it comes to wrapping them. If he is not good at folding paper and tying bows, he puts his presents in a gift bag. And he always removes the price tag.

———

A gentleman does not need to ask someone what that person wants for any special occasion. If he pays attention to the likes and dislikes of the people around him, he will already know the right thing to do.

————

If a gentleman wants to give a gift to someone he does not know very well–maybe an uncle who lives in another city–he asks his parents for their advice.

————

A gentleman does not give bad gifts to anyone. Not even his sister.

————

A gentleman knows his dad's favorite cologne and his mom's favorite authors. He also knows what type of movies they like.

Chapter 19

ANSWERING THE TELEPHONE

If you are old enough to use the phone, you are old enough to use it the right way.

There may be three guys you hang out with who don't care how you come across on the phone. Everyone else—from your parents to their friends, to your aunts and uncles, to your grandparents, to girls—does care. And they notice. Right after one of your parents' friends compliments you on your excellent telephone manners is the perfect time to hit up your parents for a later curfew, a new video game, or your own cell phone. But the best reason to use the phone the right way is because it shows people that you are a great guy who does his best to treat people in a respectful way.

You do

Speak clearly and pleasantly.

You don't

Groan as if answering the telephone were the most painful thing you ever had to do, or as if answering this call were a horrible inconvenience. Even if you think it is.

Why

A gentleman is always at his best, not just when it is convenient.

You do

Answer the phone by saying, "Hello," "Hello, this is Jason" (if that is your name), or "Hello, this is the Johnson residence" (if Johnson is the last name of the people who live at the house).

You don't

Say, "Huh?" or "Speak to me," or "What?"

Why

You want people to know whom they're talking to and whether they've dialed the right number.

You do

Put the phone down quietly, if the call isn't for you, and then find the person whom the call is for.

You don't

Yell for your mom across the house. If there's some really good reason you can't leave what you were doing—and watching television is *not* a really good reason—you should put the phone on mute before shouting into the next room.

Why

Your hollering will disturb the other people in your house, and the person on the other end of the line may suffer severe hearing loss.

You do

Be careful what you say when you answer the phone.

You don't

Tell the caller your dad can't talk right now because he is using the bathroom.

Why

Because your dad will be mad, and because he will have so many chances to embarrass you later in life.

It's best just to say, "He can't come to the phone now." You say that because it's the truth and because nobody wants to think about your dad using the bathroom.

You do

Try to be careful to punch in the correct phone number. If you do make a mistake, you say, "I am sorry, I must have dialed the wrong number."

You don't

Hang up without saying, "I'm sorry."

Why

It is rude to interrupt somebody without apologizing. The person will probably call you back, and your parents will answer the phone, and then you will be *really* embarrassed.

You do

Only call 911 for a big-time emergency. A "big-time emergency" is something like an accident or a fire. But it can also be a moment when you think something strange is going on around your house—like when you think maybe someone is trying to break in.

You don't

Call 911 if the problem isn't big-time serious. For example, if your sister throws a baseball and hits your arm, you can wait until your parents get a chance to deal with the bruise—and with your sister. If she hits you in the head and you are having trouble seeing or standing, however, you'd probably better call 911.

Why

If you call 911 for a problem that is not an emergency, you might be preventing someone else from getting the help he or she really needs. But whenever you think the situation is serious, go ahead and call 911. That is what it is for.

A gentleman puts the phone back on the charger when he is finished.

———

A gentleman does not monopolize the phone.

———

A gentleman does not eat, or slurp his drink, while he is on the phone.

———

A gentleman does not eavesdrop on other people's conversations.

————

A gentleman does not give out other people's numbers without their permission.

————

A gentleman does not call other people late at night or early in the morning.

Chapter 20

TAKING PHONE MESSAGES

Allow yourself to daydream for a moment. Ten years from now, a phone call comes in. Someone, let's say your evil little sister, answers the call. It could be the Atlanta Braves calling to tell you to report to spring training. It might be Harvard telling you they need to ask you a question before they can send your acceptance letter. It could even be a potential date calling to tell you that they will go to the prom with you. What if your evil little sister doesn't write down the message and forgets to tell you? Obviously, you could be stuck with a bad job and a bad school, and stuck without a date to the prom.

Maybe this scenario is a little extreme, but you have to treat every phone call you answer for the other members of your family like it was a call that could change somebody's life. You should write down the message and make sure to leave it someplace where it will be seen. Every call may not be as important as that call from Harvard, but it is not your job to decide how important a message might be.

You do

Ask if you can take a message when the caller asks to speak to someone who isn't home.

You don't

Give out more information than necessary. When someone calls and asks to speak to your mother, you don't say, "My mom has gone to the office, so I'm the only one here."

Why

It is never a good idea to volunteer unnecessary information, especially to a stranger.

You do

Write the message down. If you aren't sure how to spell a name, you ask the caller to spell it for you. Then you put the message in the place your family has designated as "message central." You don't just stick it in your back pocket.

You don't

Assume you will remember the message without writing it down. (Remember when you promised to take out the garbage and clean your room and write a note thanking your Aunt Louise for the underwear she sent you for your birthday?) When you get busy, it's easy to forget things. Just write the message down.

Why

You may forget to give the message to the person who's supposed to get it. For instance, if you forget to tell your sister that a boy has called to ask her to go to a dance, he may think she is stuck-up and doesn't like him. Then your sister won't have a date and your parents might make you take her—and you know how awful that would be.

A gentleman uses his best handwriting when taking messages, especially when writing down telephone numbers.

———

A gentleman does not write down messages on walls or furniture or tablecloths, just because there is no paper close by. If he must leave the phone while he searches for paper, he asks the caller to hold on a minute.

———

A gentleman does not ask for information that is not his business when he takes a message. For instance, he does not ask, "Why would you be calling my dad?"

Chapter 21

USING A
CELL PHONE

Congratulations! You convinced your parents that you needed your own cell phone and are responsible enough to have one.

Now don't mess up. And don't become one of those people who causes other people to wish that cell phones were never invented.

A cell phone can be a great thing. But it can also lead some people to forget their basic manners and annoy others.

Be sure to turn off your cell phone, or at least put the setting on vibrate, any time you really don't have to use it. That means you turn it off in movies, in theaters, in restaurants, at concerts, and at school. You even turn it off when you are just hanging out with your friends, unless there is a chance your parents will be trying to get in touch with you.

You do

Follow your school's rules governing the use of cell phones.

You don't

Download a ringtone adults are not supposed to be able to hear so you can break the rules.

Why

School rules exist for a reason: Cell phones can disrupt class. Also, if you break the rules, the school may confiscate your phone, and that will not make your parents happy.

You do

Be respectful of others, even if your cell phone starts ringing, or alerts you of a text message.

You don't

Ignore the person you are talking with in order to make a call, receive a call, or send a text message.

Why

It is rude to expect other people to stand around and wait while you are talking or texting someone else on your cell. If you must answer your phone, you should simply tell the caller that you will have to call them back later. The only exception is a call that turns out to be a real emergency, or if it is your parents calling. If you are receiving a call that you think might be important, simply get up and leave the theatre or the table, as quietly as possible.

You do

Talk as quietly as you can when using your cell phone, especially when other people are close by.

You don't

Talk so loudly that other people can hear everything you are saying.

Why

Other people probably do not want to hear your conversation. (Nobody wants to hear why you can't go to the mall. And you don't want anybody else to hear that you can't go to the mall because you left the toilet seat up and your little brother fell in and got stuck.) Keep your cell phone calls, and all your other personal conversations, to yourself. When you shout into your cell phone, you irritate other people, because you are invading their space. If the person you are talking to is having trouble hearing you, simply move away from other people, so you can speak up without intruding on the people around you.

You do

Respect the limits your parents set for your cell phone usage.

You don't

Whine when your parents take your phone away after you didn't abide by their rules and restrictions.

Why

You respect the limits your parents set, especially if they are paying the bill. Even if you are paying the bill yourself, they still get to set the limits. If they have told you that you can't use your phone at school, and you get busted, be prepared to face the consequences.

You do

Use your phone to text, play games, listen to music, and even make calls—but only when it does not bother other people.

You don't

Text or use your phone in the movie theater.

Why

Even though you may not be making any noise at all, the light from your phone will disturb those sitting around you. If a gentleman must check a message, send a text, or make a call, he goes to the lobby of the theater to do so.

A gentleman limits his data usage to the plan allowed by his parents or his wireless plan.

———

A gentleman knows that a cell phone is a luxury and a privilege. He does not use it to try to impress other people. He does not belittle other people who do not have cell phones.

———

A gentleman under no circumstance uses his phone to photograph or make a video of someone in an embarrassing situation.

———

A gentleman does not engage in loud cell phone conversations while standing in line in public places or while waiting for the bus. He does not shout into his phone as he walks around.

———

A gentleman keeps up with his cell phone. Even the most generous parent wearies of replacing lost or broken cell phones.

Chapter 22

WINNING WELL

D o you suppose that LeBron James was a bad winner when he was a boy? Did he make fun of the players on the losing teams and the other kids who weren't as talented as he was? Of course he didn't. And neither did Tom Brady, Mookie Betts, and Cristiano Ronaldo, and most of the truly great sports champions. They were lucky enough to have parents and coaches who taught them that being a good winner is as important as winning the game.

You can be the best at baseball or soccer or spelling bees or video games. But if you make those against whom you are competing feel bad, they are not going to want to play with you, or against you—not because you are better than they are, but because you take all the fun out of the game. If you take all the fun out of the game, even if you win all the time, people won't want to play on your team.

Bye-bye to fun—which is what competition is supposed to be all about.

YOU DO

Say, "Good game," to the other team or the person you are competing against.

YOU DON'T

Say, "Loser," or "Sorry you played such a lame game," or anything else that might make your competitor feel bad.

Why

You are going to lose one day yourself, and when that happens, you won't want to be treated poorly. Bragging about yourself or insulting the losing team simply makes others feel bad, and it makes you look bad. Other guys' parents are not going to want their kids to be around you. What's more, your own parents are going to be so embarrassed they may deny you belong to them.

YOU DO

Say, "Thank you," when someone compliments your skill.

You don't

Say, "I could have done better," or "I was holding back," or anything other than "Thanks."

Why

A gentleman knows how to accept a compliment. Being a good winner does not mean you can't celebrate your victory. It is right for you to enjoy your success. But it is also expected that a gentleman knows how to celebrate his success without making the other players feel inferior.

A gentleman knows that being a good winner also means having good sportsmanship.

———

A gentleman knows how to accept a compliment about a game well played.

Chapter 23

LOSING WELL

"Losing builds character."

———

"Losing makes you try harder
the next time."

———

"You'll never be a loser if you always give
it your best effort."

L et's be honest. Losing stinks.

We all know that because we've all lost before, and we will probably lose again. However, you will also win again at something—hopefully, more times than you lose.

But whether you're competing in baseball, chess, spelling bees, student council elections, or the Olympics, how you lose is really just as important as how you win.

Nobody likes the guy who claims that the other guy or the other team was lucky or cheated or that he just let them win. That kind of guy is going to be one lonely person.

You want to be the guy who, when he loses, will congratulate his opponent, even if he or she did just get lucky or even if the referee did make a bad call or even if you didn't give your best effort. When you get home, you can put all your anger and frustration into making yourself a better third baseman or chess player or high jumper. You will become a better athlete and competitor, and you will be a person whom others will want to compete with.

YOU DO

Say, "Good game," or "Congratulations," to the winner of any competition in which you've been involved.

You don't

Give up because you lost. If you are just playing to win, you are missing out on the true meaning of competition.

Why

No one wants to lose. But, if you tried hard and had a good time and learned something and spent time with some good people—you've still had a positive experience.

A gentleman does not throw a fit when a call does not go his way or when he loses.

———

A gentleman does not stop making the best effort halfway through a competition, even if he thinks it is obvious he is going to lose.

Chapter 24

HOW TO ACT IN PLACES WHERE YOU ARE BORED

Every gentleman, at some time or another, is going to be in a place where he is bored. It is a part of growing up. It doesn't just happen to young guys; it happens to adults as well. If you are smart, you will start learning how to cope with a boring situation. Otherwise you will simply make the situation worse. Whether it is a play, a wedding, a fiftieth anniversary party, a dinner in a fancy restaurant with a bunch of adults, or a really boring science class, you are going to have to go places that you don't find all that exciting or very much fun. There's nothing wrong with being bored. But it is wrong to act bored and hurt other people's feelings. Knowing the difference is often what separates the gentlemen from the immature kids.

You do

Try to keep your eyes focused on the stage at a play or a concert that your parents have made you attend.

You don't

Squirm in your seat so that everybody sitting close to you knows you are bored.

Why

You do not want to distract other people from enjoying the performance. Many of them may actually want to be there. Your parents may not enjoy going to all your ball games, but they'd never let you know it. Try to put yourself in their place.

You do

Know that even the most boring experience of your life will be over before too long.

You don't

Sigh and continually check your watch or repeatedly ask, "How much longer before we can go? Do we have to stay for the whole thing?" You may think you're making the time move more quickly, but you're only making the situation worse.

Why

You will be letting people know that you are not mature enough to handle the situation. If you can sit quietly though an incredibly boring experience, people will respect you for your grown-up manners, not to mention your patience.

YOU DO

Find ways to occupy your mind in situations where you are bored.

YOU DON'T

Occupy yourself in ways that distract others, such as cracking your knuckles or whispering or humming to yourself.

Why

Not everybody else is bored, just because you are. Your dad may think you're actually enjoying the ballet. He doesn't have to know what's really going on in your mind.

A gentleman does not assume that his own boredom gives him permission to distract those around him.

———

A gentleman does not hurt the feelings of others by complaining about his boredom, before, during, or after an event.

————

No matter how bored he may be, a gentleman never whines.

————

A gentleman does not chew gum in church, in the theater, or at the table.

Chapter 25

HOW TO BEHAVE IN A MOVIE THEATER

Which is worse?

1. Talking to your friends during a movie.
2. Talking back to the screen during a movie.
3. Talking on your cell phone during a movie.

Obviously, this is a trick question. All three of them are rude, ungentlemanly ways to behave. Any one of them can ruin the movie-going experience for the rest of the audience.

There's one simple reason people spend their money to go to a movie: They expect to have fun. They do not expect to have to listen to the conversations of the people sitting around them. The only people they want to hear talking are the people up on the screen.

Even your friends will think you're obnoxious if

you continue to talk, rustle your popcorn, or slurp your soda during the movie. The next time you say, "Want to go with me to a movie?" they may simply tell you, "Sorry. Maybe another time."

Make sure to demonstrate to your friends that you can enjoy a movie without disturbing other viewers. Otherwise, you may find yourself having to go alone.

You do

Turn your cell phone off—or at least turn off the ringer or put it on vibrate when you go to a movie.

You don't

Assume that your telephone call is so important that it can justify ruining the movie for others.

Why

No call you receive is that important. If a gentleman really needs to answer a call, he gets up from his seat and doesn't start talking until he's reached the lobby.

You do

Feel free to laugh when something is funny, or scream when something is scary. It is also okay to cry when something is sad.

You don't

Feel free to talk with your friends about what is happening on the screen.

Why

Screaming and laughing are part of the fun of going to the movie. It is not cool, however, to give your opinion of the movie while other people are trying to watch it.

A gentleman stops talking as soon as the movie begins.

———

When a gentleman arrives at a movie that has already begun, he enters as quietly as he can and tries to find a seat as quickly as possible. He does not roam up and down the aisle, disturbing other people.

———

There are times when a gentleman must speak during a movie—for example, when he asks his friend to pass the popcorn. However, he keeps his comments as brief, and as quiet, as possible.

————

A gentleman knows that watching a movie at home is different from watching a movie in a theatre. At home, he and his friends can hit the pause button to talk or take a bathroom break. There is no pause button in a movie theatre.

Chapter 26

TRAVELING ON AN AIRPLANE

Maybe you have taken a lot of airplane trips, or maybe a flight is yet in your future. Maybe you usually fly with your parents or with other adults, or maybe you're facing the challenge of traveling by yourself.

Traveling on an airplane is exciting, no matter how many trips you've taken before. No matter how excited you are about taking the trip or reaching your destination, the rules for being a gentleman still apply. They may even be *more* important on an airplane, where you are in a small space with a lot of people, or in an airport, where there are even more people—all of them in just as big a hurry as you are.

You do

Follow the instructions of the security personnel in the airport, and pay attention to the flight attendants on the plane.

You don't

Make jokes about bombs or explosions or plane crashes. And you don't complain about having to take off your shoes, and your belt, and your jacket, and your cap before you go through the security checkpoint. The people at the security checkpoint didn't make the rules, so complaining to them will only make you seem childish. What's more, it won't do any good, and it will just slow down the process and make it take even longer for you to get to your destination.

Why

There's nothing funny about a bomb or a plane crash, and you should realize that there are serious penalties for joking about bombs in airports.

You do

Respect the people sitting near you. If you talk, keep your voice down. If you want to talk to a friend seated in one of the rows in front of you, don't shout. In most cases, it will be best to hold off on that type of conversation until the plane has arrived at the airport.

You don't

Play your music or your video games or watch a DVD without using your headphones.

Why

The people near you may be trying to read, rest, or get some work done. Flying also makes some people nervous. Loud talking or loud noises may only make them more uneasy.

When traveling on a plane, a gentleman does not kick or bump the seat in front of him.

———

A gentleman says, "Excuse me," when he must slip past the passengers seated next to him in order to leave his seat, even if one of those passengers is his brother or his sister.

————

A gentleman does not throw his candy wrappers or other trash on the floor of the airplane. When a flight attendant comes down the aisle with a trash bag, he tosses his candy wrappers, soda cups, and old magazines into the bag.

————

Unless he needs to use the restroom, a gentleman stays in his seat, with his seatbelt buckled. He stays out of the aisle.

Chapter 27

WALKING IN FRONT OF OTHER PEOPLE

There are three types of people in the world:

1. People who show up early.
2. People who show up on time.
3. People who show up late.

Unless you are one of the people who shows up early, you are going to have to walk in front of people when you go to a movie, to the theatre, to a ball game, or any other place where people are seated in rows.

Unless there is enough room for you to walk directly to your seat, you will have to walk in front of the people who showed up earlier than you. You can do this one of two ways—either with your rear end in their faces, or facing them.

This is a no-brainer. People don't want to look at your rear end. They would rather see your face.

You do

Say, "Excuse me," as you move down the row—especially if you're making somebody shift around and make room for you.

You don't

Say, "I'm sorry," unless you've stepped on somebody's feet.

Why

You only say, "I'm sorry," when you have done something wrong. You say, "Excuse me," when you are merely inconveniencing someone.

You do

Everything in your power to show up on time.

You don't

Be the one in your family who causes everyone to be late.

Why

Being late is inconsiderate—not only to your family, but also to all the other people who are going to be interrupted as you step over them on the way to your seat.

A gentleman is careful not to step on the toes or feet of other people as he walks to his seat.

———

If other people must move down the row where a gentleman is seated, he makes it easier for them by rising from his seat.

Chapter 28

RESPONDING TO INVITATIONS

Parties are a great way to have fun with your friends, a great way to make new friends, and a perfect way to celebrate special occasions.

When you were younger, your parents knew about all of the party invitations you received. But now those party invitations are probably coming directly to you. Sometimes a friend will simply say, "My birthday party is next Saturday. Can you come?" Other invitations will be written and will come to you through the mail, or as an e-mail.

Either way, it is important for you to respond to the invitation as quickly as possible. (If you or your parents have ever hosted a party, you know how important it is for the hosts to know how many people to expect, so they can have enough food for everybody.) If a friend simply invites you to a party face-to-face, it might be best for you to say, "That sounds like fun. Let me check with my parents."

A gentleman may not want to go to every party to which he is invited. But even though it is fine for him to say no, he makes sure he does not hurt another person's feelings. He never says, "Don't count on me. I'll probably have something better to do," or "I don't think so. That doesn't sound like much fun to me," or "I don't know if I want to go. Who is going to be there?"

Instead, he simply says, "I'm sorry but I won't be able to make it to your party. Thanks for the invitation." There's no reason to say anything else.

There are two different types of written invitations. Here is how you deal with each type.

You do

Nothing, if the invitation says, "Regrets only"—unless you are not planning to attend. "Regrets only" simply means "Let us know if you're not going to be there. Otherwise, we'll be expecting to see you." If you are not planning to go to the party, you must call the host and let him know you won't be attending.

You don't

Wait until the day before the party to decide whether you will attend.

Why

The hosts are probably already counting on your being there. Just think what it would be like if ten people waited that late before they declined the same invitation. That could mean four or five large pizzas going to waste.

You do

Call and let the hosts know whether you are planning to attend the party, if the invitation says "RSVP." (RSVP is short for *répondez s'il vous plaît*, which is French for "please respond.") There will probably be a deadline for responding to the invitation. Be sure to reply before the deadline has passed.

You don't

Simply assume your hosts won't care if you just show up.

Why

It is very inconsiderate not to respect the deadline for replies to a party. Of course, there's always the chance that an emergency will come up and keep you from attending. People understand when that happens. But they will have a harder time understanding if it appears that you've simply changed your mind at the last minute—or if you were simply too lazy to respond to the invitation by the deadline.

A gentleman feels free to accept or decline a party invitation by e-mail if an e-mail address is provided.

Chapter 29

USING A NAPKIN

What we are talking about here are napkins that are made out of real cloth. This is the type of napkin you will find in most restaurants where the drinks are served in real, breakable glasses. Your mother probably wants everybody to think your family uses cloth napkins—even if you really use paper towels most of the time, except when you have company. But regardless of what type of napkin you are using, the rules are pretty much the same—except that you never put a paper napkin in the washing machine.

Knowing the right way to use a napkin should be a no-brainer. You just use the napkin to wipe your hands and your mouth, and then you're done, right? But it's not that easy. What do you do with your napkin when you need to stand up from the table?

What about when you are finished with your meal?
And what if you drop it?

Fortunately, you are old enough, smart enough,
and cool enough to learn the rules.

YOU DO

Put your napkin in your lap as soon as you sit down at
the table.

YOU DON'T

Tuck your napkin into your shirt.

Why

People will think you don't have good manners
and it will embarrass those who love you most. What's
more, if you tuck your napkin into your shirt, it will
look like you are wearing a bib.

YOU DO

Use your napkin to wipe your hands and your mouth.

YOU DON'T

Use your napkin to blow your nose.

Why

If you blow your nose in your napkin, there is a really good chance you will have to use it again. Gross. If you need to use a tissue or handkerchief, ask for one or excuse yourself and head for the restroom.

You do

Put your napkin in your seat when you have to leave the table for any reason during the meal.

You don't

Put your napkin on the table, if you're planning to come back.

Why

The other people sitting at your table don't want to look at your dirty napkin while they are trying to eat.

You do

Put your napkin on the table when you are leaving the table at the end of the meal.

You don't

Put the napkin in your chair or on your plate when you are finished eating.

Why

When you put your napkin on the table, it means you are finished with your meal. If you are in a restaurant, it means the server can go ahead and start removing the dirty dishes.

A gentleman does not worry if he drops his napkin on the floor. He picks it up and quickly puts it back in his lap.

———

If the napkin has become soiled while it was on the floor, however, he asks for a clean one.

———

A gentleman may find himself in some restaurants where the server will place the napkin in his lap for him. If this happens, a gentleman tells the server, "Thank you."

Chapter 30

USING THE CORRECT FORK

Sometimes, when you come to the table—
especially at the holidays, or in a fancy
restaurant—you will find a lot of forks set out in
front of you. You may want to ask, "Hey, what's the
deal with all the forks? Is somebody just trying to get
me to mess up?"

Relax. Forks are no big deal. Most of the time,
there will be only two of them. You use one of them
(the smaller one) to eat your salad, and you use the
other one to eat the rest of your meal. If there are a lot
more forks on the table, just do what the adults do.
Saying, "Hey, I'm just a kid," is not your best defense.
If you don't want to be treated like a kid, try not to act
like one.

Unless the person who set the table has got it
wrong, the forks will always be set in the same way:

The salad fork will be on the outside. The dinner fork will be on the inside, next to the plate.

That makes sense, because you eat your salad first, so your salad fork is the first one you pick up. When it comes to choosing the correct fork, always start with the one on the outside. When you're finished with that fork, use the next one. If you start on the outside and work your way in, you'll always be safe.

When you are finished with your salad, you put your salad fork on your salad plate, and leave it there.

When you are finished with your dinner, you put your dinner fork on the plate, alongside your knife.

When it comes time for dessert, you will probably be offered a clean fork with which to eat it—especially if you're eating in a restaurant. If you're eating at somebody else's house, however, and if they don't offer you a new fork, just watch the adults at the table and do what they do.

YOU DO

Put your fork on your plate if you must set it down. While you are eating, you put it on your plate.

You don't

Put your fork back on the table after you have used it.

Why

A dirty fork gets food on the table or the tablecloth.

You do

Be cool if you accidentally start eating your salad with your dinner fork.

You don't

Freak out and make a big deal about it. Most likely, no one will notice.

Why

Everybody makes mistakes. People will have more respect for you if you keep your cool when you make a mistake—especially a little one, like picking up the wrong fork.

And finally, just one more time, to make sure you've got it right: When it comes to using your forks, you start from the outside and work your way in toward your plate. Stick with that one rule, and you'll be doing the right thing the whole way through dinner.

If a gentleman drops his fork on the floor, he asks for a new one to replace it.

———

If a gentleman comes to the table and finds that his silverware has been wrapped in a napkin, he unrolls the napkin and sets the forks in their correct places.

Chapter 31

USING A KNIFE AND FORK

There are two ways to use your knife and fork. One is called the American style. The other is called the Continental style. Either one is correct, so you get to figure out which one works best for you.

In the American style, you start with your fork in your left hand and your knife in your right. After you have cut off a bite of food, you put your knife down on your plate. (You only cut the bite you are going to eat right then; you do not cut up your entire steak at one time.) Then you move the fork from your left hand to your right hand before you put the bite of food in your mouth.

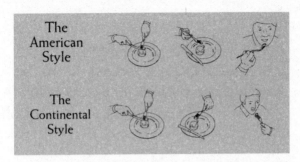

The American Style

The Continental Style

In the Continental style (Continental means it was invented in Europe), you keep your fork in your left hand all the way through the meal. You still cut your food the same way, as in the American style. The only difference is that after you put down your knife, you don't move the fork to your right hand.

Again, either style is fine. It's your choice. When it comes to good manners, there may not be many times when you're given a chance to choose what you want to do. So choose your knife-and-fork style wisely.

YOU DO

Put your knife and your fork on your plate after you have used them.

YOU DON'T

Put your knife, your fork, or any other utensil back on the table after you've used it.

Why

Dirty utensils make a mess of the table.

A gentleman may ask for a steak knife
at a restaurant.

———

A gentleman never asks for a steak knife
at a private home, if he has not been
offered one. Such a request is a not-very-
nice way of saying "The meat you have
served me is tough."

———

A gentleman does not use his dinner
knife to cut the butter, if a butter
knife has been provided.

Chapter 32

REFUSING FOODS YOU CAN'T EAT

There are perfectly good reasons why some people can't eat certain foods. A lot of people have allergic reactions to foods such as shellfish, nuts, or even dairy products. The reactions might make them sick. And some reactions can even be fatal. Some people also decline to eat certain foods because it is against their religious beliefs.

If you are one of these people, you probably already know it, and your parents probably keep close watch on the food that is served in your house or the food that is ordered when your family goes to a restaurant. But your parents are not with you every time you sit down at the table. When you're visiting a friend's home, having dinner with your soccer team after practice, or even eating at the school cafeteria, you may sometimes be offered foods that you simply cannot, or do not, eat.

The situation can sometimes be a little awkward. For example, when you're at your best friend's house for dinner, you may discover that his mother is serving barbecued shrimp—and you are allergic to shellfish. You don't want to insult your friend's mother, but you don't want to spend the night in the emergency room, either.

It would be wrong for you to risk your health to avoid hurting someone's feelings. So your only option is to tell your friend's mom, as nicely as possible, that you cannot eat shrimp because you have a food allergy or because your family does not eat shrimp. There is no reason to give any more details.

You may be able to avoid this situation, however, by letting your friend know in advance that there are things you cannot eat.

You do

Tell your buddy, when he invites you over for dinner, that you can't eat fish or peanuts or cheese—whatever it is that you cannot eat. It might even be a good idea for your mom or dad to call your friend's parents beforehand, so they can discuss your dietary restrictions.

You don't

Wait until you sit down at the table at your friend's house to announce that there are foods you cannot eat.

Why

Your friend's family wants you to have a good time and enjoy your meal. If they haven't been made aware of your dietary restrictions, they will be disappointed, and you may end up going home hungry.

You do

Say, "I'm afraid I'm allergic to shellfish, but these potatoes and green beans look great."

You don't

Expect your friend's parents to go back to the kitchen and prepare a separate meal for you. They aren't running a restaurant, after all.

Why

A gentleman would never keep the rest of the family from proceeding with their dinner. Just for once, it won't hurt you to ask for a second helping of green beans.

A gentleman never gives in to peer pressure to try something that he knows he couldn't or shouldn't eat.

Chapter 33

DEALING WITH FOODS YOU DON'T LIKE

Some guys will eat anything. They will eat squid or liver. They will eat Thai food or Mexican food or Chinese food or Indian food. You name it, they'll eat it. They would probably eat dirt or worms if somebody served it to them.

Life may not be that easy for you. You may be the type of guy who would prefer to live off nothing but chicken fingers and pizza, with french fries as the vegetable course. That doesn't mean, however, that you still can't act like a gentleman at mealtime.

There will be a time when you're going to go to a restaurant that doesn't serve chicken fingers. Or you will be sitting down for dinner at a friend's house and be served Brussels sprouts. When that dilemma arises, you could try to get out of the situation by saying, "I'm sorry. I'm allergic to Brussels sprouts." But it's unlikely anybody will buy that excuse—especially your mom or dad.

You do not have to eat Brussels sprouts, especially if the very sight of them makes you sick. But you will have to learn how to turn down dishes you don't like, without hurting somebody else's feelings or throwing a tantrum at the table.

You do

Say, "I think I'll pass on the okra. This corn looks great. I'll have more of that, please." But you only need to say that if somebody asks you why you're not eating the okra. If nobody raises the question, simply pass the bowl along to the next person and enjoy the corn.

You don't

Say, "I don't like okra. It makes me vomit."

Why

Nobody at the table wants to hear you talk about what makes you sick. Just proceed to enjoy the dishes you do like, so it will be clear to your host that you are having a great time.

You do

Sample a small portion of a dish you have never tried before.

You don't

Assume you must finish the entire serving, if you hate it. You never try to hide what you didn't eat under a lettuce leaf or a piece of bread. And you never try to stuff it in your napkin. Simply leave the uneaten food on your plate.

Why

Your host will give you credit for at least trying the dish. Adults know that not everybody likes every type of food. It is childish to turn up your nose at a dish you've never even tasted.

You do

Attempt to find something on the menu you think you will like, if you find yourself in a restaurant that doesn't serve the food you usually eat.

You don't

Complain to the people who have taken you to a Mexican restaurant that Mexican food is the only thing on the menu.

Why

The people who have brought you to this restaurant obviously like it and figured you would like it, too. It is not cool, when you're already at the table, to announce that you hate everything on the menu. If your hosts do ask you to be part of the decision-making process when it comes time to choose a restaurant, it is perfectly fine for you to say, "I'm not a big fan of Mexican food," if that's what they are suggesting.

A gentleman never spits out food that he has put in his mouth just because he doesn't like it.

————

A gentleman does not remove uneaten food from his mouth unless it is, for some reason, inedible. If he encounters a piece of bone or gristle or something that is blistering hot, he removes it in the most discreet way possible.

————

A gentleman knows that the worst thing he can say to his host or hostess is, "This doesn't taste good."

Chapter 34

ORDERING FROM A MENU

There was a time when, if your parents took you to a restaurant, they took you to one where all your favorite foods were on the menu. You could order chicken fingers, macaroni and cheese, a grilled cheese sandwich, a hot dog, or even a slice of pizza. Life was just the way you wanted it to be.

Those were the days, however, when you could still get away with ordering from the kids' menu. But you're older now, and your days with the kids' menu are over.

When you go to a restaurant now, you'll be offered the same menu the adults use and you'll be expected to order for yourself. That may seem like a scary prospect, but it's scary for a lot of adults as well.

Sometimes, when they look at a menu, they see lots of unfamiliar dishes. Many times, the restaurant doesn't offer any of their favorite foods. But they survive, and so can you. You can work your way through any menu, if you remember a few tips.

You do

Remember that the server is your friend—a friend who wants you to enjoy your meal. Maybe that's because the server hopes somebody at the table will leave a great tip. Or maybe he or she simply wants you and your friends to come back to the restaurant again.

You don't

Pretend that you understand everything on the menu because you think it makes you look cool. If there's something on the menu that you've never heard of or something you don't understand, ask your parents to explain it. If they don't know the answer—and they may not—feel free to ask your server, "Could you tell me what calamari is? Would you tell me what chanterelles are, please?" (Just so you know, calamari is squid; chanterelles are mushrooms.)

Why

The way you learn new things is by asking questions. You aren't the first person who didn't know what calamari is, and you won't be the last. Don't be afraid to ask questions.

YOU DO

Ask for something to be prepared a slightly different way, if you wish.

YOU DON'T

Assume that you are the first person who doesn't like onions, or olives, who has eaten at that restaurant.

Why

Everybody at the restaurant wants you to have a good time and to enjoy your food. You don't want to get a reputation as a picky eater, but a minor change, such as leaving the onions off a sandwich, is no big deal in most restaurants.

A gentleman is not afraid to speak up if his meal has not been prepared the way he requested it. If he asked for his steak to be cooked well done and it is served medium rare, he politely brings the mistake to the server's attention. When the server says, "Let me get that corrected for you," a gentleman says, "Thank you very much."

———

A gentleman waits until the others at his table have been served before he begins eating. If there is a lady at the table, he waits until she begins eating before he begins.

Chapter 35

HOW TO USE CHOPSTICKS

I f you find yourself at a restaurant that serves Asian food, you may discover that a pair of chopsticks is the only eating utensil provided.

The use of chopsticks is not a complicated maneuver. Here is a simple guide.

1. Place one chopstick in the crease of your thumb.

2. Brace the other chopstick against your middle finger.

3. Use the two chopsticks, as if they were tweezers or pliers, to pick up bite-sized portions of food, dip them in soy sauce or other condiments, and then pop them into your mouth.

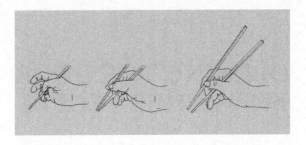

Using chopsticks may seem difficult, but you can handle them. After all, guys all over the world use them all the time. It may take a little practice, but before long you'll find that you can master using chopsticks—the same way you can do any other thing you put effort into.

If a gentleman feels uneasy about trying to use chopsticks, he asks for a knife and fork instead. He would rather eat his meal without dropping his food than try to use equipment he hasn't mastered yet.

Chapter 36

OPENING THE DOOR FOR OTHER PEOPLE

When you open the door for another person, here are some of the nice things you can expect to hear:

"Thank you."

"I hope my son does that."

"Aren't you nice?"

"What a gentleman!"

And sometimes, when people say these things, your mom or dad will hear them—and that will be very good for you. But even if your folks never hear about all the nice things you do, doing nice things for other people will make you feel great.

Holding the door open for other people and letting them walk ahead of you—at the mall, in church, or even at school—is one of the nice things you can start doing right now. It doesn't matter if the

other person is your age or the age of your grandfather.
A gentleman holds the door open for women and men,
young and old.

You do

Open the door for someone you see coming right
after you.

You don't

Stand there and hold the door open if the person is a
considerable distance away.

Why

It is polite to hold the door open for anyone
walking in behind you, but if a person is far away and
sees you standing and waiting, they may feel the need
to rush and walk faster than usual.

You do

Hold the door open for a group of people who are
walking in together.

You don't

Decide that you've done your duty, after half the
group has walked in, and let the door slam in
somebody's face.

Why

Being a gentleman is about doing nice things for other people. It won't kill you to hold the door open for a few extra seconds. Usually someone in the group will say, "Thanks," and offer to take over for you.

If a gentleman is walking a short distance behind a lady, he steps forward to open the door for her.

————

If a gentleman is walking a long way behind a lady, he does not rush forward to open the door—unless he sees that the lady is carrying a number of packages and may have difficulty managing the door on her own. He may say to her, "May I open the door for you?"

————

If a gentleman opens the door for someone who does not say, "Thank you," he does not mention that person's lack of manners. A gentleman never calls attention to another person's thoughtlessness.

Chapter 37

A GENTLEMAN GOES ONLINE

Y ou are lucky. You are part of a generation of people who have known about computers ever since they were born. For older generations, computers were science fiction; but you probably use them every day— either to do your homework or to have fun. Because you've been around computers all your life, you may take them for granted. But when you take them for granted, you run the risk of abusing or misusing one of the greatest inventions of all time.

You may already be at a time in your life where you spend a lot of time online. It could be playing games, listening to music, doing research for your homework, or visiting the website or blog for your favorite athlete or influencer. But as you get older, you will probably spend even more time online on things like social networks, sending and receiving e-mails, and managing your schedule. Just remember this: You are not an anonymous guy sitting behind a computer screen. Treat your online life just like you do your real in-person life. Treat others with respect, be courteous, and do not give out too much information.

You do

Follow the rules your parents or your teachers set for computer use.

You don't

Give out personal information on your computer to people you don't know. If you give out information to strangers, you may be putting yourself or your family at risk.

Why

You really don't know the person you might be talking to in a chat or direct message. The Internet is a great way to meet new people, but you must be cautious. Respect the boundaries your parents set for your computer use—and use common sense.

You do

Use your head and remember your manners when you are sending e-mails or instant messages or posting comments.

You don't

Send any dirty or questionable e-mails or instant messages to anyone. Although you might think a dirty joke is funny, your friends—or, more important, their parents—might not want that sort of communication coming into their home.

Why

You don't want to be known as "The Boy Who Sends Dirty E-mails." And you definitely do not want your own parents getting angry calls from your friends' parents. After that type of phone call, you could find yourself grounded, with all your computer privileges revoked.

You do

Know that there are times when a phone call or an in-person conversation is better than an e-mail.

You don't

Hide behind an e-mail when you have to say
something difficult.

Why

A gentleman is never cowardly. It may be
uncomfortable to tell a girl face-to-face that you can't
take her to a dance, but it would be unkind simply to
send her an e-mail saying "Sorry. I can't take you to
the dance." Even if you don't like her very much and
you figure the dance will be boring, you do not want
to hurt her feelings. It's part of your job as a gentleman
to treat other people with respect and help them feel
better about themselves. People will appreciate it
when you make that effort in person.

You do

Use your head when it comes to responding to e-mails
from people you don't know. (It may be a good idea
not to respond to them at all.)

You don't

Ever share private information such as your social
security number, your birthdate, your banking
information, or your home address with anyone online
without your parents' permission.

Why

There are people out there who will use your information in ways that can lead to big trouble. You might think that answering an e-mail to get a free iPad is a great idea. Always remember that whenever you see something that seems too good to be true—especially if you see it online—it usually is. Use your head, so you don't fall for these sorts of tricks.

You do

Pay for the music and movies you download.

You don't

Try to steal movies and music without paying.

Why

Does anybody need to tell you why stealing is wrong? But even if that weren't enough, this kind of theft could get your parents sued for a lot of money—and cause you to lose all your Internet privileges.

You do

Use the Internet to learn things that can help you with your homework.

You don't

Copy things from an online source and try to pass them off as your own work.

Why

There is a big word for this kind of stealing. That word is "plagiarism," and it could mean earning an "F" if you get caught. (And you probably *will* get caught.) It could also get you kicked out of school for an honor violation. It is fine to use a reliable online source for research. Just make sure to take what you have learned and put it into your own words.

You do

Respond in some way to friend requests on social media.

You don't

Have to accept every friend request you receive.

Why

You don't have to accept friend requests from people you hardly know or don't even know at all. All you have to do is hit the "ignore" or "delete" buttons.

You do

Know there is a difference between sending a private message and posting a message.

You don't

Post information that you don't want a lot of other people to see.

Why

Just as you don't go around broadcasting everything you say to everyone you meet, there are probably private things you want to say online. Always make sure you are sending your message to the people you want to receive it—and to nobody else.

You do

Share photos and news on your social media page.

You don't

Share embarrassing photos of yourself and others with negative comments on your page.

Why

Once you post a photo, a lot of other people will see it; and you will probably never be able to take it back. Sometimes, however, a photo you think is funny can really be hurtful or insulting to another person. Think of all the embarrassing photos that have been taken of you. They may have seemed funny at the time, but how would you feel if someone posted them online for everyone to see?

A gentleman does not use his computer to say bad things about other people.

———

A gentleman does not create an e-mail address that is in bad taste.

———

A gentleman does not do anything on the computer that puts himself or his family at risk. This includes talking to strangers and illegal downloading.

Chapter 38

BORROWING AND SHARING

You've been hearing about borrowing and sharing ever since you were a baby. Your parents or your babysitter probably taught you that you should share your toys with others and that you should let your sister have some of the cookies, too.

As you get older, however, sharing your own stuff and borrowing things from other people take on a new meaning. That's because some of the stuff you have now is more expensive than the toys you played with when you were little. What's more, you now have stuff that has a lot more personal meaning to you. You have stuff that you plan to keep for a long time, and it's important to you.

It's likely that the things you'll be asking to borrow from others will be more valuable, too. As you get older, when you ask to borrow anything, you will want to be more and more responsible. You will also learn that some people do not take good care of the things they borrow. If a friend has a history of damaging or losing your property, it is okay to tell him or her no. In fact, it is the smart thing to do.

You do

Take care of anything you borrow (and that includes a book or a DVD you borrow from the library).

You don't

Treat another person's property as if it isn't worth much—even if it doesn't seem very valuable to you.

Why

Your buddy's old, worn-out catcher's mitt might have a special meaning to him—a meaning you don't know about. It may have been a gift from his grandfather, who used to play in the minor leagues. Think how bad you would feel if you lost something that was a gift from your grandfather—a gift that could never be replaced.

You do

Know there are some things you should never share or lend.

You don't

Let someone borrow your property, just because you want them to like you.

Why

If a friend asks to borrow your favorite fishing pole—a fishing pole that cost a bundle and was a very special gift from your parents—it is okay to say no, since you know it probably can't be replaced. Likewise, if a friend asks to borrow your gaming system when he goes on vacation for a week and you know you won't want to be without your video games for that long, it is okay to say no. Although it is okay to say no, you must still say it like a gentleman. A gentleman would never say, "No, you can't borrow it. I'm afraid you will break it." A gentleman would simply say, "I'm sorry, I can't lend my fishing pole. It was a gift from my parents." And that is all you have to say.

You do

Accept someone else's decision when you ask to borrow something.

You don't

Whine or beg when someone tells you no.

Why

Begging is never cool. Pleading, "But I promise I'll take good care of your gaming console. I really, really promise," only makes you sound like a baby. Put yourself in the other person's shoes. There is probably a good reason he or she has said no. At the same time, your friend's game console is his property. He doesn't have to lend it to you, unless he wants to. When a friend tells you no, you respect his decision and figure out another way to enjoy music during your vacation.

If a gentleman breaks something he has borrowed, he finds a way to replace it or to repair it.

―――――

A gentleman does not borrow anything that he can't afford to replace or repair. He thinks twice before asking to borrow an expensive item.

―――――

A gentleman knows the difference between saying no for a good reason and being selfish. He avoids being selfish, at any cost. A gentleman tries to help others out in every way he possibly can.

Chapter 39

THE UNZIPPED ZIPPER AND OTHER EMBARRASSING SITUATIONS

I t's funny when . . .
- People slip on some ice and fall on their rear ends.
- A guy laughs so hard that milk comes out of his nose.
- A guy walks around school or at a party with his pants unzipped.
- A guy's voice cracks while he is giving a report.

But it's not funny when you're the guy who falls on his rear end, when milk comes squirting out of *your* nose, when *you* are the guy walking around with his fly open, or when *your* voice cracks in front of a crowd of people.

Actually, some other people *may* think it's kind of funny, but it may not seem all that funny to you.

From time to time, every guy will discover that he is walking around with his fly open. And people fall down on the ice all the time. The voice-cracking thing will eventually end. And the milk thing usually happens when you are laughing at something that's really funny.

You are going to have a much better life if you are able to laugh along with your friends when you do something embarrassing or funny.

A gentleman tries his best not to let such moments bother him.

You do

Tell another guy if you notice that his zipper is open.

You don't

Point at the other guy in front of other people and call unnecessary attention to the fact that his zipper is open. And you do not make lame remarks such as,

"Hey, Bobby, looks like the barn door is open."

Why

A gentleman always puts himself in the other fellow's place. He knows that, if he were the one walking around with his zipper down, he wouldn't want anybody making fun of him.

You do

Understand that other people may not share your sense of humor. It may not be a good idea to laugh out loud when somebody falls on an icy sidewalk. Other people may not think it's as funny as you do.

You don't

Get so caught up in laughing that you forget to ask the person who fell if he or she is hurt.

Why

A person can get seriously hurt by a fall. But even if he or she is not seriously hurt, it is your duty as a gentleman to help him or her up and make sure he or she is not seriously injured.

If a gentleman sees somebody walking around with a piece of toilet paper stuck to his or her shoe, he tells that person about it, very quietly.

————

If a gentleman has seen someone walking around with a piece of toilet paper stuck to his or her shoe, he does not go around telling the story to other people.

Chapter 40

BOUNDARIES: YOURS AND THEIRS

Doors are good.

Doors with locks are even better.

But knowing how to knock on a closed door is the best.

Everyone needs, wants, and deserves some privacy in his or her life. That's why doors come in handy.

When you were three years old, it probably didn't bother you if people walked in while you were in the bathroom. The door to your bedroom was probably unlocked all the time. As you've grown older, your feelings have probably changed, and your privacy is probably a lot more important to you. Well, guess what? Just as you want some privacy every now and then, so do the other people in your home. You're not a three-year-old anymore, and your parents and sister don't want you barging into the bathroom without knocking first.

You do

Respectfully ask your family members to knock before entering your bedroom or opening the door to the bathroom.

You don't

Yell, "Can't you knock?" when someone walks in on you without asking. It probably isn't necessary for you to put a "Do not disturb" sign on your bedroom door. In most cases, it will do the trick if you simply say, "Mom and Dad, I'd appreciate it if you'd knock before coming into my room," or "If you think I might be in the bathroom, please knock before opening the door." If that doesn't work, you can always lock the bathroom door.

Why

You are not a little boy anymore. It is okay for you to request your own personal space and to ask to have some time alone. If you explain that to your parents, more than likely they will understand and cooperate.

You do

Know that if you spend thirty minutes in a locked bathroom, people are going to want to know what's taking so long.

You don't

Hog a bathroom that you share with other people.

Why

A gentleman understands that the family bathroom is not his private hideaway.

You do

Show your family and your friends the same respect that you would like them to show to you.

You don't

Barge into their rooms when the door is shut, or even knock on the door, if you think they may be trying to have some private time.

Why

Your parents and your brothers and sisters need privacy every now and then, the same way you do. If you respect their boundaries, they will be much more likely to respect yours.

A gentleman never asks anyone, "What were you doing in there? Why did you lock the door?"

———

A gentleman never opens a closed door without knocking first and waiting to be invited to come in.

Chapter 41

TAKING PRIDE IN YOUR APPEARANCE

Being dressed right doesn't always mean being dressed up. You don't need to wear your best clothes when you are mowing the yard or playing football or going fishing or just hanging around the house. But that doesn't mean you don't take pride in your appearance. Nevertheless, a gentleman understands that there will often be special occasions—such as a meal in a restaurant or a party—when he will want to pay special attention to the way he looks.

Looking good doesn't mean that you have to wear the most expensive clothes. But it does require that you make sure your clothes are clean and pressed, that they are appropriate for the occasion, and that they go together.

Not every guy is good at knowing what to wear. If you are one of those guys, you don't have to worry, since there are plenty of people out there who will be glad to help you out. The important thing is that you do your best to look your best.

You do

Learn how to use an iron.

You don't

Just wear a wrinkled shirt because nobody else had the time to iron it for you.

Why

It just takes a few minutes to make the difference between looking good and looking like a slob. Ironing is not rocket science. It's not even as tough as the first level of a video game.

You do

Ask if you are not sure whether a shirt looks good with a pair of pants, or if a tie goes with a suit.

You don't

Feel ashamed if you can't match colors.

Why

It's a fact that millions of guys are color-blind. If you need help, ask for it—if you are actually color-blind or if you just have trouble matching up your clothes. It beats having people think that you don't care how you look or laughing at you for wearing a black sock and a blue sock at the same time.

You do

Accept the fact that there are some times when you are going to have to wear a suit or a tuxedo or some other stuffy outfit that you'd really rather not wear.

You don't

Whine or complain or mope when you have to get dressed up.

Why

Trust us, you'd rather put on the tux for the wedding and deal with it than be the only guy your age dressed like a little kid.

If a gentleman plans to attend an event that has a dress code, he follows it. (The dress code will be included on the invitation to the event.) If he does not understand what the dress code means (if it says "black tie," for example), he asks to have it explained.

———

A gentleman does not wear stained clothes.

———

A gentleman does not wear ripped or torn clothes, except at casual occasions. Even if he has paid a lot of money for a pair of jeans that were ripped and torn when he bought them, he does not wear those jeans at a dressy party.

———

A gentleman buckles his belt at his waistline. He does not let the waistband of his pants or jeans slip down over his hips, and he does not let his underwear show in public.

Chapter 42

TYING YOUR OWN TIE

Let's face it. There are going to be times when you will have to wear a tie. At some point you are going to go to a wedding, a funeral, a fancy dinner, or maybe even a play or a concert where a tie will be required. (Some guys even have to wear a tie to school—every day.) For men of all ages, wearing a tie is like paying taxes. It's just something you have to do.

If it is tied correctly, the tip of the tie should come right to your belt. Not three inches above it. Not six inches below it. If you don't get it right the first time, try again. Until you know how to get it right the first time, give yourself lots of time to practice in front of a mirror.

Just say no to clip-on ties. If you are old enough to be reading this book, you are old enough to tie your own tie. Even if your parents try to talk you into wearing a clip-on tie, tell them that you think you are man enough to start tying your own tie.

Here are the steps to tying your own tie. You know how to reach the tenth level in a video game. This is a lot easier than that. So don't even start the "this is too hard for me" bit.

Four-in-Hand Knot

1. The wide end of the tie should hang down below the narrow end. Cross the wide end over the narrow end.

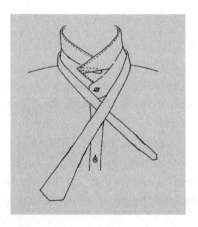

2. Bring the wide end under and then over the narrow end.

3. Bring the wide end under the narrow part of the tie.

4. Bring the wide end of the tie through the knot that has been created.

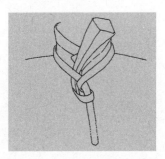

5. Pull the wide end of the tie down the front of your shirt.

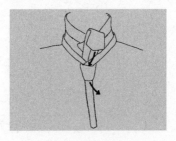

6. Tighten the knot and draw it snug to your collar.

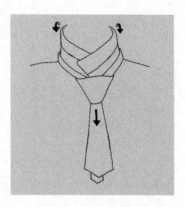

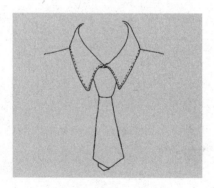

A gentleman waits until after he has brushed his teeth before he puts on his tie. If he is already wearing his tie and then remembers that he hasn't brushed his teeth, he flips the tie over his shoulder. That way, he makes sure he doesn't get toothpaste drool all over it.

————

A gentleman does not use his tie as a napkin.

————

When he is wearing a tie, a gentleman takes extra care about eating things like pasta, ice cream, and any sandwich with lots of mustard or ketchup on it.

Chapter 43

SHINING YOUR SHOES

If somebody asks you if you've been out plowing in a field, it's probably time for you to give your shoes a shine.

You can't wear sneakers all the time. Sometimes you are going to have to wear black or brown leather shoes. And every once in a while, those shoes are going to need some attention.

People really do look at your shoes. If you keep your shoes in good shape, they will figure you care about your appearance. They will also figure that you know how to take care of your possessions. On the other hand, if you walk around in muddy, scuffed shoes, you may hear comments from your parents such as:

- "How can you take care of a puppy when you can't even take care of your shoes?"
- "How can you take care of a dirt bike when you can't even take care of your loafers?"
- "How can you take care of a car when you can't even take care of your shoes?"

Your shoes do not have to be fancy. But if you keep them clean, people will understand that you know how to take care of your property.

You do

Shine your shoes when they need it. (And they need it whenever they've become scuffed or if they've picked up mud or dirt.)

You don't

Wait until your dad or mom tells you to get out the shoe polish.

Why

You have some self-respect. You want to look your best.

You do

Get a professional shoe shine if you and your folks are at a good hotel, an airport, or some other place where shoe shine service is offered.

You don't

Assume it is uncool to sit on the shoe shine stand. In fact, people will think you *are* very cool, because they will understand that you really care about your appearance.

Why

If you watch the professional giving the shoe shine, you will see how the job really should be done. You will also be experiencing one of life's great treats.

When a gentleman shines his shoes, he puts newspaper or an old towel down on the floor around him. He knows that shoe polish can make a big mess.

———

When he's shining his shoes, a gentleman will probably get some shoe polish on his hands, so he washes them as soon as the job is done.

_____

If a gentleman gets a professional shoe shine, he tips the shoe shiner.

_____

How to Shine a Pair of Leather Shoes

The necessary equipment: Soft cloth, wax polish, water, soft brush (optional).

The procedure:

1. Sprinkle a bit of warm water over the polish. (And yes, spit works just fine.)

2. Cover a finger with the soft cloth and use it to work the water into the polish.

3. Apply the polish to the shoe.

4. Work the polish into the leather.

5. Using a clean section of the cloth (or a soft brush), buff the leather to a brilliant shine.

Chapter 44

WHEN TO TAKE OFF YOUR CAP

Baseball caps are great. They cover your head when you have a bad haircut or when you didn't feel like washing your hair. They show your support for your favorite team or your favorite store or tractor. They protect you from the sun on a hot day.

No matter how great his baseball cap may be, however, a gentleman knows there are times when he takes it off, no matter how hot the sun may be.

You do

Take off your cap when you sit down to eat.

You don't

Think that, just because you are in a fast food restaurant, you can get away with leaving your cap on. (And turning it around backwards doesn't count.) Your cap always comes off, completely, at mealtime. If you can't figure what else to do with it, roll it up and put it in your back pocket.

Why

People want to be able to see your face while they're sharing a meal with you.

You do

Know that there is a time and a place to wear a cap.

You don't

Wear a baseball cap in your classroom or in church. And you don't wear a baseball cap with your suit and tie—even if it is your favorite cap, and even if it is clean and almost brand-new.

Why

Caps are for casual times, not for times when you want to look dignified.

A gentleman takes off his cap during the National Anthem, during the Pledge of Allegiance, or whenever the American flag is passing by.

————

A gentleman takes off his cap when he is being introduced to another person— especially if he is being introduced to an older person.

————

A gentleman does not wear a cap with a slogan or a logo that might insult or embarrass another person.

Chapter 45

TAKING CARE OF YOUR FINGERNAILS

Having dirty fingernails is nothing to be ashamed of. It happens when you have been out mowing the lawn or fixing your bike or doing something else that involves hard work. It also happens when you have been playing a rough game of baseball or soccer. But after you are done with all the hard work or the hard playing and before you sit down for dinner, you have to wash your hands and pay attention to your fingernails.

You do

Clean your fingernails with the tip of a nail file.

You don't

Clean the dirt out with your teeth.

Why

You wouldn't just go out into the yard with a knife and fork and eat dirt, would you? A gentleman doesn't eat dirt. And he doesn't eat bicycle grease. That, however, is just what you're doing when you try to clean your fingernails with your teeth.

You do

Trim your fingernails and toenails regularly.

You don't

Wait until you look like Freddy Krueger or Count Dracula before you trim your fingernails. If you trim your toenails and it turns out they are long enough to use as a bookmark, you've definitely waited too long.

Why

Long fingernails aren't a good look. They get dirty more easily, and they scratch people. They are a sure sign that you don't take pride in your appearance.

A gentleman has his own fingernail and toenail clippers.

Chapter 46

HANDKERCHIEFS AND TISSUES

Wiping your nose on the back of your hand—or your shirt sleeve—is truly gross. That's why handkerchiefs and tissues were invented—to catch all the stuff that comes out of your nose and mouth when you cough or sneeze.

You never know when you are going to sneeze— or when you are going to realize that something really unfortunate is hanging from your nose. That's why a gentleman always has a handkerchief that is made of cloth, it can be washed and used again. That means, however, that a gentleman has to check his handkerchief every day, to make sure it isn't so dirty that it needs to be replaced.

You do

Have your handkerchief or tissue ready when you feel a sneeze coming on.

You don't

Wait and hope that the urge to sneeze will go away—or that it will be a fairly dry one.

Why

Catching a sneeze early is better than cleaning up afterward.

You do

Offer your handkerchief or a tissue to someone if he or she needs it—but only if it is a clean handkerchief or a dry tissue.

You don't

Offer someone a dirty handkerchief or a damp tissue.

Why

The sight of a dirty handkerchief or tissue can be really disgusting—and it can spread germs.

A gentleman washes his hands after he sneezes, especially if he has a cold.

————

A gentleman throws his used tissues in the trash as soon as he can. He does not let them pile up on his desk or, even worse, on a table at a restaurant.

————

A gentleman does not pick his nose in public.

Chapter 47

PICKING UP AFTER YOUR PET

Remember when you begged your parents to let you have a puppy? Remember how you promised, again and again, that you would take care of him and wash him and feed him and take him for walks? At that point, you probably were thinking about all the cool things you could do with your own dog—things like rolling with him in the leaves and letting him lick your face.

But owning a pet means that you have to be responsible for the not-so-fun times as well as the fun ones. And that means you have to deal with pet poop. Unless you live in the country and have a dog who goes into the woods to do his business, or you've got a cat who has figured out how to use the toilet, picking up pet poop or cleaning out the litter box is going to be part of your standard routine.

Whether you said it or not, that was part of the promise you made when you asked for a pet. It's not just a promise you made to your parents. You also made it to everybody who's likely to walk down the sidewalk after you and your dog.

You do

Pick up your dog's poop when you take him for a walk in somebody else's yard.

You don't

Leave the poop in the grass, even if nobody is watching.

Why

Other people don't want the surprise of stepping in your dog's poop, much less the burden of trying to scrape it off their shoes. Would you want other people turning your yard into the community dog poop park?

You do

Take along a plastic bag to put the poop in. You can slip the bag over your fingers like a glove. That way, you'll eliminate poop-to-hand contact.

You don't

Just toss the bag in the middle of the street or drop it in somebody else's garbage can.

Why

It's *your* dog's poop. It goes in *your* trash can.

You do

Empty your cat's litter box on a regular schedule.

You don't

Wait until your entire house smells like old kitty litter before you clean it out.

Why

Gentlemen don't live in houses that smell like old kitty litter.

You do

Clean up your dog's poop, even if he chooses to do his business on his own home turf.

You don't

Wait until someone steps in a big pile of poop and tracks it into your house, causing you to get yelled at.

Why

You don't want to spend your time cleaning the carpet. Life will be a lot easier if you just go ahead and pick up the poop.

A gentleman takes responsibility for his own pets.

———

A gentleman walks his dog regularly, allowing enough time for his dog to do his bathroom business.

———

A gentleman always carries a plastic bag or two when he walks his dog.

Chapter 48

PICKING UP
AFTER YOURSELF

You may think that, once you're an adult, you won't have to clean up after yourself. You may assume that nobody will care if you throw your socks on the floor, or that it will be all right for you to leave your dirty dishes in the sink for as long as you like, or that it will be okay if you don't clean up until somebody writes, "Clean me," in the dust on the coffee table.

Once you are out on your own, you will get to choose how often you straighten up and how often you clean the place where you live. That may sound like fun right now—but it won't be fun when your apartment starts to smell and your landlord threatens to kick you out. And it will be even less fun when your friends stop coming to your house because they're tired of tripping over your dirty clothes.

Right now, your parents probably expect you to do your part in keeping your house or apartment clean. And they are right. If you get used to being messy and tossing leftover food under your bed, you will have a much harder time breaking that habit when you get out on your own.

YOU DO

Hang up your wet towels after you've finished your shower.

YOU DON'T

Throw them on the bathroom floor.

Why

After a while, wet towels begin to smell. If you let them sit around long enough, unhealthy stuff will start growing in them and they will turn green.

YOU DO

Put your dirty dishes in the sink after you've finished eating. Better yet, you wash them, or rinse them and put them in the dishwasher.

You don't

Just leave a dirty plate or a half-eaten sandwich sitting around, even in the kitchen.

Why

Your mom and dad aren't your servants. Maybe one day you will be able to pay somebody to clean up after you. But until that day comes around, it's your responsibility to do your part to help keep your house clean.

A gentleman does not leave his shoes and jacket lying around in the place where he dropped them when he took them off. He knows that his shoes and his coat have a place and he puts them there, without having to be told to do so.

———

A gentleman cleans up his room without waiting for somebody to tell him to do so. He recognizes when things are getting out of hand and does his part on his own.

———

A gentleman knows that old food smells bad and can attract bugs or rodents. He disposes of uneaten food by dropping it in the garbage can or putting it down the disposal.

———

When the garbage can is getting full, a gentleman takes out the trash, without having to be asked to do so.

Chapter 49

PUTTING DOWN THE TOILET SEAT

There's a story about a guy who didn't put down the toilet seat. In the middle of the night, when his little brother went to the bathroom, he fell in, got stuck, and almost got flushed to death. It's not a true story, but what is true is that sitting on a toilet when somebody forgot to put down the seat is not any fun.

YOU DO

Raise the seat when you have to urinate.

You don't

Neglect to wipe off the rim of the toilet or the floor, if your aim is not so good.

Why

Who wants to look at a nasty, stinky toilet?

You do

Put the seat down when you are finished, even if you are lucky enough to have your own bathroom.

You don't

Expect every person to look before they sit down. People sometimes forget to look before they sit.

Why

It's important to form good habits. Hearing a woman scream, "Were you raised in a barn?" after sitting down on a toilet when you forgot to put the seat down is not funny.

A gentleman flushes every time he
uses the toilet.

––––––

A gentleman cleans up after
himself in the bathroom.

––––––

A gentleman knows how to scrub a toilet,
even though he doesn't like doing it.

Chapter 50

PERSONAL HYGIENE

The days are long gone when it was your parent's job to give you a bath. You are growing up and your body is changing. That may mean that, if you aren't careful, people will start noticing your body odor. If you've already detected this problem in your friends, it's probably time for you to pay more attention to your own personal hygiene. It's time to stop griping about having to take a shower.

If you want people to be able to stand being around you, you are going to have to take a shower every day—maybe even more often if you play a lot of sports and get really sweaty. You probably should go ahead and wash your hair every time you take a shower, and you may need to start wearing deodorant. What's more, you can't even think about wearing the same shirt or jeans three days in a row.

You do

Take a shower as soon as you can if you have been sweating.

You don't

Assume, just because you took a shower in the morning, that you don't have to wash up after a good basketball game.

Why

If you've been sweating, you probably smell bad.

You do

Know that it is okay to pay attention to your personal hygiene.

You don't

Want to be known as a slob.

Why

People notice how you look, and dirty hair and dirty clothes don't make a good impression. You may think you don't care if people think you are a slob, but it won't be long before you realize that you want to impress the people at the school you want to attend or the boss you want to work for.

YOU DO

Find a shampoo, a soap, and a deodorant that you like.

YOU DON'T

Be afraid to ask your mom or your dad to let you have your own stuff—especially if you don't like theirs.

Why

Your parents know that you are more likely to stay clean if you can use products that you like. They probably won't mind letting you have your own bath and shower supplies.

A gentleman knows that he can wear a baseball cap only so often. He washes his hair and gets it cut so that he is not ashamed to be seen without his cap.

———

When a gentleman thinks he can smell his own body odor, he knows that other people can smell it, too. That is when he starts using deodorant regularly.

———

A gentleman puts on a clean shirt instead of smelling the armpits of a shirt to see if he can wear it again.

———

A gentleman brushes his teeth regularly and uses mouthwash or breath mints if he thinks he even might have bad breath.

INDEX